North Nor[folk]
R[ailway]

Alan Price

Contents

NORTH NORFOLK RAILWAY

First published in 2018

British Library Cataloguing in Publication Data

A catalogue record for this book is available from the British Library.

ISBN 978 1 85794 519 5

Silver Link Publishing Ltd
The Trundle
Ringstead Road
Great Addington
Kettering
Northants NN14 4BW

Tel/Fax: 01536 330588
email: sales@nostalgiacollection.com
Website: www.nostalgiacollection.com

Printed and bound in the Czech Republic

Title page: **SHERINGHAM** Former LMS Stanier Class 5 4-6-0 No 45337 is seen leaving Sheringham with a mixed goods train. This was one of the most prolific classes of steam locomotive to run on the railways of Britain; in excess of 800 were built from 1934 onwards and they became known as 'Black Fives'. No 45337 has just negotiated the level crossing that allows road access to Sheringham golf course.

Introduction

Engineer William Marriott led the construction work on the line between Melton Constable and Cromer, part of which forms today's preserved North Norfolk Railway. The line opened to traffic in 1887 and became part of the newly formed Midland & Great Northern Joint Railway (M&GN) in 1893. Upon the grouping of the railway companies in Britain in 1923, unusually the M&GN remained independent, not being absorbed into the London & North Eastern Railway (LNER) until 1936. Railway nationalisation in 1948 saw control of operations pass into the hands of British Railways, which finally closed the line in 1964 under its rationalisation plans.

The Midland & Great Northern Joint Railway Society was formed in 1959 at a time when closure of much of the M&GN network was well under way. The aims were to preserve the memory of the M&GN in East Anglia, where there was much affection for the former Melton Constable-based company.

Eventually the North Norfolk Railway became established, with the Midland & Great Northern Joint Railway Society as a major shareholder, and rebuilding of the line began in 1965.

Today the society is the custodian of no fewer than five locomotives based on the railway, together with other items of rolling stock and artefacts, and is very much part of what has made the North Norfolk Railway the success it undoubtedly is today.

Sheringham

Below: **SHERINGHAM** The North Norfolk Railway's largest station is viewed here from the east, the station is the headquarters of the modern-day preserved railway. Although many of the buildings have been adapted to serve these requirements, in appearance they still exude the atmosphere of times past, decorated in the colours of the British Railways Eastern Region era.

Right: **SHERINGHAM** A replacement footbridge at the eastern end of the platforms was reinstated in June 2016 the original having previously been removed. In this busy scene during the 2016 Autumn gala GER 'Y14' No 564 awaits departure from Platform 2. *David Mitchell*

SHERINGHAM LEVEL CROSSING 11 March 2010 was a very special day in the preservation story of the North Norfolk Railway, marking the official opening of the new level crossing between Sheringham East, the single-platform terminus station on the national rail network, and the North Norfolk Railway's historic station, which first opened to traffic in June 1887. Suitably wearing 'The Broadsman' headboard, No 70013 *Oliver Cromwell* led a special excursion train from London King's Cross station to Sheringham, where Pete Waterman officiated as the train became the first to cross the resort town's Station Road in 46 years, arriving at precisely 2.21pm.

The two shots on this page show the 'Britannia' 'Pacific' arriving with its train, and the hordes of people who turned out to savour the atmosphere on this most momentous of days.

Above: **SHERINGHAM** Wearing Great Northern Railway livery, Gresley 'N2' Class 0-6-2 tank locomotive No 1744, which dates from 1921, makes a departure from Sheringham, with *Oliver Cromwell* awaiting its subsequent departure with the special train from King's Cross. The 'N2' is the only preserved example of its class, and is seen here during a lengthy spell on the East Anglian line. The train, comprising the articulated 'Quad-Art' coaching stock, which is based on the North Norfolk Railway, is also unique in preservation today.

Right: **SHERINGHAM WEST SIGNAL BOX** controls train movements at Sheringham station, and stands just beyond the Church Street road bridge, under which trains pass as they pull away from the station. Although occupying the same position as its predecessor, the box is not original to the site; of Great Eastern Railway (GER) design, it formerly stood at Wensum Junction, Norwich, and was moved to the North Norfolk Railway following its decommissioning in 1982. The 31-lever frame within the box was rescued from the redundant Leyton Station signal box in London.

Left: **SHERINGHAM WEST SIGNAL BOX** On this occasion the 'Quad-Art' coaches are seen behind the 1912-built Great Eastern Railway Worsdell 'Y14' Class 0-6-0 No 564, resplendent in its smart GER blue colour scheme.

Below left: **SHERINGHAM** Hauling the first ever excursion train to pass on to the North Norfolk Railway from the national network, *Oliver Cromwell* makes its departure from Sheringham bound for the line's current terminus at Holt. There have been thoughts about making a link from Holt to the Mid Norfolk Railway, but any developments of this ambitious idea, if practical, are certainly well in the future.

Below: **SHERINGHAM** British Railways Standard Class 4 2-6-0 No 76084 dates from 1957 and represents a much later period of steam locomotive design in Britain. The range of Standard locomotives arrived in the early 1950s and represented a move towards the modernisation of the fleet as a means of updating the whole railway scene following nationalisation in 1948, which had become necessary following the heavy toll inflicted on the network during the war years.

The signal is set for departure of the train; the West signal box is just out of sight beyond the Church Street road bridge.

Left: **SHERINGHAM** The GER 'Y14' prepares to depart from Sheringham's No 1 Platform. Built at the GER's Stratford Works, No 564 became part of the London & North Eastern Railway fleet when the GER was absorbed under the grouping of Britain's railway companies in 1923. In LNER days the 'Y14' Class was reclassified as 'J15', and the running number 7564 was adopted. Following nationalisation, the locomotive became No 65462, and following withdrawal from service the 0-6-0 entered preservation in 1963 and became the only survivor of 289 class members built between 1883 and 1913.

Below left: **SHERINGHAM** A second sole survivor of its class that can be found enjoying a life in the preservation era is former LNER 'B12' Class 4-6-0 No 1572. Passing under the road bridge, it makes a departure for a trip along the line.

Below: **SHERINGHAM** Another British Railways Standard locomotive, 9F 2-10-0 No 92203, makes a departure. The 9Fs were built primarily for heavy goods train duties, but did find their way onto passenger train turns. This example often carries non-authentic *Black Prince* nameplates, a name that was adopted when the 2-10-0 passed into the ownership of the renowned artist David Shepherd. Today the 9F is the largest and heaviest member of the North Norfolk Railway steam locomotive fleet.

SHERINGHAM Four further images of the Great Eastern Railway 0-6-0 show the locomotive at Sheringham.

In the first (*above*) it is seen leaving with the 'Quad-Art' articulated stock. Built at Doncaster in 1924, Set No 74 is the only surviving example of this style of coaching stock. The design was developed during Nigel Gresley's time as the Great Northern Railway's Carriage & Wagon Superintendent for use by the GNR to ferry commuters in and out of London.

The North Norfolk Railway can also boast other impressive examples of vintage coaching stock, some of which are seen behind No 564 (*above right, right and above far right*) as it stands ready to leave Sheringham, then passes under the Church Street road bridge.

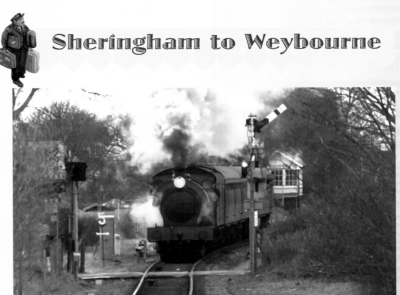

Above right: **SHERINGHAM GOLF COURSE LEVEL CROSSING**
Leaving Sheringham, 0-6-0 saddle tank *Ring Haw*, built by the Leeds-based Hunslet company in 1940, approaches the level crossing that gives road access to Sheringham Golf Club. The 0-6-0 spent its working life at Nassington ironstone quarry, near Peterborough, prior to arriving at the North Norfolk Railway in 1970. Smaller industrial locomotives like this were used extensively on heritage lines in Britain during the early years of railway preservation and it is somewhat refreshing to see that the East Anglian line is still able to run an engine representative of that era alongside the much larger main-line examples more readily seen today.

Right: **SHERINGHAM GOLF COURSE LEVEL CROSSING** A diesel-hauled passenger train works away from the crossing and passes the lineside sign that indicates to approaching locomotive crews that a 10mph speed restriction is in place over the crossing.

total of nine survived the cutter's torch following withdrawal of the class between 1964 and 1968, barely 14 years after the first of the class had emerged from the works. In 1960 9F No 92220 *Evening Star* became the last steam locomotive to be built during the steam era in Britain.

However, more recently No 60163 *Tornado*, constructed from scratch by the A1 Steam Locomotive Trust, now actually holds the distinction, in the short term at least, of being the final standard gauge steam locomotive built in Britain … so far.

SHERINGHAM TO WEYBOURNE

Both of these shots show the same train as it starts away from Sheringham, hauled by British Railways Standard 9F 2-10-0 No 92203 *Black Prince*. Although not visible here, the nameplates are in place on the smoke deflectors.

The 9Fs were built at Crewe and Swindon between 1954 and 1960, with a total of 251 examples eventually entering traffic. No 92203 was built at the former Great Western Railway's Swindon Works and became part of the British Railways fleet in 1959. It saw fewer than ten years in service before passing into preservation in 1967. A

SHERINGHAM TO WEYBOURNE Sole surviving 'B12' Class 4-6-0 No 8572 is now seen twice with the same train, comprising the 'Quad-Art' coaching set, as it works away from Sheringham shortly after crossing the golf course access road. The main picture shows just how closely the road into the town runs beside the railway at this location.

Right: **SHERINGHAM TO WEYBOURNE** This is the second Swindon-built 9F 2-10-0 to feature in this book. Numbered 92214, it was a visitor to the North Norfolk Railway from its Great Central Railway base at Loughborough. While *Evening Star* was the only class member to be named during British Railways days, this particular locomotive was named *Cock O'The North* in 2011, a name that had once been carried by a Gresley 'P2' Class 2-8-2 locomotive. No 92214 also carries the Brunswick Green livery that was only ever applied to one class member, No 92220 *Evening Star*, in recognition of its place in history as the last steam locomotive built by British Railways.

Left: **SHERINGHAM TO WEYBOURNE** Type 2 diesel-electric locomotive No D5631 hauls a mixed goods train away from Sheringham. These locomotives were built at the Brush works in Loughborough, and under the TOPS numbering scheme became known as Class 31. No D5631 was supplied new to Norwich shed in 1960 and today forms part of the collection of locomotives preserved under the M&GN Joint Railway Society banner.

Right: **SHERINGHAM TO WEYBOURNE** A steam locomotive far away from its original Great Western Railway stamping ground is '5600' Class 0-6-2 tank No 5619, seen during a visit to the railway in 2012. The train is rounding the curve shortly after leaving Sheringham, with the 18-hole golf course just visible on the left.

Above: **SHERINGHAM TO WEYBOURNE** British Railways 'Standard 4' 2-6-0 No 76084 is owned and cared for by the 76084 Locomotive Company Ltd, and the summer of 2013 saw the 'Mogul' (a term given to a locomotive with a 2-6-0 wheel arrangement) return to steam thanks to a partnership forged with the North Norfolk Railway that enabled the completion of the restoration. It carries main-line certification, which, due to the opening of the level crossing at Sheringham in 2010, makes it a very important part of the North Norfolk Railway-based locomotive fleet; in recent times it has been used on 'Cromer Diner' services. Here it is seen working light engine away from Sheringham on its way to the locomotive shed at Weybourne following a day's work hauling trains along the line.

Right: **SHERINGHAM TO WEYBOURNE** The Sheringham fixed distant signal is about to be passed by visiting '4900' 'Hall' Class 4-6-0 No 4936 *Kinlet Hall* as it rounds the curve on the approach to the first climb faced by trains as they make their way along the line bound for Weybourne and Holt.

SHERINGHAM TO WEYBOURNE Two further trains are seen at the same location as *Kinlet Hall*. The first (*above*) is headed by ex-LMS Stanier 'Black Five' 4-6-0 No 45407, built in 1937 by Armstrong Whitworth & Company. It is starting the climb away from Sheringham during a visit to the railway in 2013.

Built in 1962 at the Vulcan Foundry, English Electric Type 3 diesel-electric locomotive No D6732 (*right*) looks splendid in its 1960s Brunswick Green livery. Later, under the TOPS numbering system, these locomotives became known as Class 37, and this locomotive became No 37032.

SHERINGHAM TO WEYBOURNE The M&GN concrete signal post that carries the fixed distant signal is a prominent feature in this image, capturing 'B12' 4-6-0 No 8572 with the 'Quad-Art' coaching stock. The concrete signal posts found all around the Midland & Great Northern Joint Railway system were produced at the company's Melton Constable headquarters.

SHERINGHAM TO WEYBOURNE The 'Quad-Art' coaches feature once again in this shot as the GER 'Y14' Class (LNER 'J15') 0-6-0 starts to climb, having passed the distant signal.

SHERINGHAM TO WEYBOURNE

Simply oozing typical early-1960s railway atmosphere, No D6732 makes a powerful image as it climbs away from Sheringham with the carmine-and-cream-liveried British Railways Mk 1 coaching stock in tow.

Left: **SHERINGHAM TO WEYBOURNE**
Today based at the Llangollen Railway in North Wales, 'Black Five' No 45337 spent some time as part of the North Norfolk Railway fleet of steam locomotives. Here in 2015 the former London Midland & Scottish Railway classic 4-6-0 makes the initial climb away from Sheringham.

Below: **SHERINGHAM TO WEYBOURNE**
9F 2-10-0 No 92203 is seen without its *Black Prince* nameplates in an almost identical position, but on this occasion the wind is blowing the exhaust towards the coast. Although the whole train is not visible in the shot, it is formed of several of the railway's Mk 1 coaches in order to provide a more authentic length of passenger train for this locomotive class, in contrast to the more usual shorter trains found on the line.

Left: SHERINGHAM TO WEYBOURNE No 92203 is captured again from a more head-on viewpoint. Working a passenger train of a more standard length, there are only four coaches and a goods van in tow, so no real strain for a locomotive that packs as much punch as No 92203 with its 9F power rating. The *Black Prince* nameplates are once more on the smoke deflectors, together with 'The Norfolkman' train headboard.

Main image: **SHERINGHAM TO WEYBOURNE** 'Black Five' No 45407 is seen at the same place but from the opposite side of the line.

Above: **SHERINGHAM TO WEYBOURNE** Very much a flagship locomotive for the North Norfolk Railway, the smart looking Apple Green-liveried 'B12' climbs away from Sheringham with its exhaust swirling down over its train and almost hiding the fact that it consists of no more than five vehicles.

Above right: **SHERINGHAM TO WEYBOURNE** In much duller conditions, British Railways Standard Class 4 tank locomotive No 80072 heads the same train formation, consisting of the articulated coaching set together with a 1929-built LNER Pigeon Van.

Right: **SHERINGHAM TO WEYBOURNE** The Great Eastern Railway 0-6-0 of 1912 heads a train made up entirely of truly vintage vehicles dating from a similar period around the early years of the 20th century. It is true to say that there are not many current heritage lines that can put together a complete train from a similar period of British railway history, and those that can deserve a salute for their dedicated work towards preserving an era of rail travel that is now part of our distant past.

SHERINGHAM TO WEYBOURNE There are only two surviving ex-LNER Edward Thompson-designed 'B1' Class 4-6-0s from a total of 410 locomotives that were built between 1942 and 1952, their construction being continued by British Railways into the post-nationalisation years. No 61306, seen here, was built in 1948 and delivered new to British Railways. The livery carried here is representative of the transition period following nationalisation, with the LNER Apple Green colour scheme but the new BR running number and 'British Railways' spelled out on the tender sides. The name *Mayflower* was never carried by this engine during its BR years, although long-since-scrapped classmate No 61379 was given the name. No longer forming part of the North Norfolk Railway fleet, No 61306 did spend some time based on the line.

SHERINGHAM TO WEYBOURNE The sole surviving 'B12' 4-6-0 is seen at the same location, tackling the initial climb after leaving Sheringham.

SHERINGHAM TO WEYBOURNE 9F 2-10-0 No 92214, in its non-original Brunswick Green livery, carries the 'Hook Continental' train headboard. This service once ran between London Liverpool Street and Harwich Parkeston Quay, connecting with the night ferry bound for Hook of Holland.

Above left: **SHERINGHAM TO WEYBOURNE** Just about to enter the cutting on the climb away from Sheringham, the 'B12' is captured on mixed goods train duties.

Above: **SHERINGHAM TO WEYBOURNE** This side view of a double-headed train shortly after it has cleared the cutting shows the sea in the background on a section of the line that can often be very bleak when a harsh wind blows inland.

Left: **SHERINGHAM TO WEYBOURNE** As trains emerge from the cutting they encounter a foot crossing, which is suitably accompanied by a Midland & Great Northern Joint Railway cast-iron lineside sign, representing the historical background of the line.

SHERINGHAM TO WEYBOURNE No 564 is accompanied by the 'Quad-Art' set together with the LNER Pigeon Van, which is often used in trains made up of the articulated teak-panelled coaches, making a fine eye-catching sight.

THE NORTH NORFOLK RAILWAY ROUTE MAP

HOLT Passing the signal box, a train arrives at Holt station, built by the North Norfolk Railway.

Sheringham
(NNR)

Weybourne

Right: **WEYBOURNE** The Weybourne outer home signal is passed shortly before trains arrive at the station, the only crossing point between Sheringham and Holt.

Kelling Heath Halt

HOLT The town's original station no longer survives, and the NNR facility is located at High Kelling, just short of the market town itself.

KELLING HEATH HALT
Shortly after departing from Weybourne, a train is about to pass Kelling Heath Halt non-stop.

Holt

To Melton Constable (closed)

Right: **WEST RUNTON** The station retains the once familiar nameboard which dates from the age of steam.

heringham
(reateranglia)

West Runton

Above right centre: **WEST RUNTON** The Guard checks that all passengers are safely on or off the train before giving the right away signal to the driver.

Below: **SHERINGHAM** 'Class 156' No 156402 is seen at the terminus of the national network line from Cromer and Norwich on 16 September 2017.

Cromer

Above: **CROMER** The friendly Guard on 'Class 156' No 156402 gives a thumbs up on Saturday 16 September 2017 prior to departing for Norwich.

Cromer High (closed)

Cromer Links Halt (closed)

To Mundesley-on-sea (closed)

Roughton Road

To North Walsham, Norwich and the National Network

Left: **Roughton Road** Many of the wayside stations throughout the country are tended by local support groups and this is in evidence at Roughton Road and other stations along the route. 'Class 156' No 156402 is seen again about to depart for Norwich. *All this page Peter Townsend*

Left: **SHERINGHAM TO WEYBOURNE** Shortly after emerging from the cutting that follows the climb away from Sheringham, this train is headed by one-time North Norfolk Railway-based 'Black Five' No 45337. The sea provides a backdrop, and the freshly cut crop in the field indicates that it is harvest time, late August or early September – the shot was taken during the Autumn Steam Gala of 2015.

Below left: **SHERINGHAM TO WEYBOURNE** Viewed from an angle much closer to the running line, the home-based British Railways Standard 9F 2-10-0 is also captured having just hauled its train through the cutting.

Right: **SHERINGHAM TO WEYBOURNE** Perspectives are very much shortened in this image of the former Great Western Railway '5600' Class 0-6-2 tank locomotive. The M&GN concrete-post distant signal is seen way back behind the train, while in the middle distance is a cast-iron lineside sign at a foot or occupational crossing. Just ahead of No 5619 a 'whistle' board warns crews on the footplate of Sheringham-bound trains to sound their whistle as a warning on approaching the crossing.

Right: **SHERINGHAM TO WEYBOURNE**
Great Central Railway-based Gresley 'N2' Class 0-6-2 tank locomotive No 1744 is teamed up with the articulated coaching stock as it approaches the end of its climb away from Sheringham.

Right: **SHERINGHAM TO WEYBOURNE**
The GWR '5600' Class 0-6-2T crests the summit of the climb from Sheringham, and it's time for the driver to ease back on the regulator as No 5619 heads downgrade towards Weybourne.

Above: **SHERINGHAM TO WEYBOURNE**
The British Railways Standard Class 4 'Mogul' has just drawn its train of carmine and cream BR Mk I coaching stock over the summit. Because the locomotive carries the early style of British Railways emblem on its tender it is perfectly suited to be teamed up with these coaches. BR painted its coaching stock in what was termed by enthusiasts as 'blood and custard' up to the mid-1950s, after which the all-over darker maroon livery, similar to that formerly used by the LMS, became standard except on the Southern and Western Regions.

Above right: **SHERINGHAM TO WEYBOURNE** At the head of a train of mixed vintage coaches, the 1912 Great Eastern Railway 0-6-0 has just crested the summit and will shortly pass under a three-arch bridge.

Right: **SHERINGHAM TO WEYBOURNE**
The suburban 'Quad-Art' coaches make up the train on this occasion as No 564 is captured having just passed under the bridge.

Overleaf: **SHERINGHAM TO WEYBOURNE**
Bathed in glorious evening sunlight, visiting Great Western Railway 'Hall' Class 4-6-0 No 4936 *Kinlet Hall* runs along the embankment after passing under the bridge and exiting the cutting.

Above: **SHERINGHAM TO WEYBOURNE**
Earlier in the day than the previous picture, the home-based 'B12' 4-6-0 is seen leaving the cutting with its train and emerging onto the embankment, with the North Sea very prominent in the background.

Right: **SHERINGHAM TO WEYBOURNE** At the end of a busy day hauling service trains along the line, No 5619 is seen on the embankment as it works light engine towards the locomotive shed at Weybourne.

Left: **SHERINGHAM TO WEYBOURNE**
British Railways 9F No 92203 is seen without its *Black Prince* nameplates, which have been removed for a photographic charter specially arranged to feature the 2-10-0. On emerging from the cutting onto the embankment, trains now begin to climb again on the 1 in 80 gradient as they head for Weybourne.

Right: **SHERINGHAM TO WEYBOURNE**
Shortly before crossing the main Sheringham to Weybourne road, 'Black Five' No 45337 is captured on the embankment. These Class 5 4-6-0s were a William Stanier development of the Great Western Railway 'Hall' Class 4-6-0, refined by him when he moved from the GWR to the LMS to take up the post of Chief Mechanical Engineer on 1 January 1932. This shot shows the 'Black Five' in action in 2012. Note at this time that no British Railways tender-side emblems are carried.

Above and above right: **SHERINGHAM TO WEYBOURNE** No 45337 is seen again in 2015, with the tender-side emblems now being carried, as the 4-6-0 draws its train along the embankment (*left*), then approaches the bridge crossing the Sheringham to Weybourne road, which is just visible on the extreme left.

Right: **SHERINGHAM TO WEYBOURNE** Working tender-first, the resident 'B12' 4-6-0 crosses the road bridge as it heads for Sheringham in order to commence its duties working service trains along the line.

Below: **SHERINGHAM TO WEYBOURNE** During the same light-engine movement as that seen on the facing page, No 8572 progresses along the embankment with the four-sail Weybourne windmill prominent in the background. The windmill dates from 1850 and regularly features in photographs of trains in action on the North Norfolk Railway.

Right: **SHERINGHAM TO WEYBOURNE** Now hauling its first train of the day, the 'B12' passes the windmill once more as it heads for Weybourne.

SHERINGHAM TO WEYBOURNE Due to a harsh wind off the sea, the coaches behind the 'B12' are almost hidden as the teak-panelled articulated four-coach set is drawn across the bridge.

Below left: **SHERINGHAM TO WEYBOURNE** Less windy conditions here as the 'Quad-Art' coaches together with the Pigeon Van are seen behind the Great Eastern Railway 'Y14' Class 0-6-0.

Below: **SHERINGHAM TO WEYBOURNE** Two Apple Green-liveried locomotives take charge of this double-headed train. The LNER version of the colour scheme is carried by the leading 4-6-0 locomotive, No 8572, while 'B1' 4-6-0 No 61306 sports the interim, early British Railways Apple Green livery.

Left: **SHERINGHAM TO WEYBOURNE** Great Western steam power now, with the visiting '5600' Class 0-6-2 tank locomotive crossing the road bridge.

Below: **SHERINGHAM TO WEYBOURNE** This is certainly a case of 'super power', with not one but two 9F 2-10-0s combining forces at the head of the train. No 92203 *Black Prince*, which was purchased from David Shepherd in 2015, is the leading, or pilot, locomotive, while the Great Central Railway-based No 92214 is the train engine.

Above: **SHERINGHAM TO WEYBOURNE** Dating from the latter years of steam locomotive production in Britain, the BR 'Standard 4' mixed-traffic 'Mogul' No 76084 entered traffic in 1957, having been built at Horwich Works. Supplied new to Lower Darwen shed in March 1957, the 2-6-0 was withdrawn from traffic in December 1967 and, with little more than 10½ years in service, went to Dai Woodham's famous Barry Island scrapyard. It was subsequently rescued from there and entered preservation in January 1983. It is highly unlikely that this class of locomotive would ever have worked in combination with 'Quad-Art' coaching stock during its days with British Railways.

Right: **SHERINGHAM TO WEYBOURNE** The Great Eastern Railway 'Y14' Class 0-6-0 heads towards Weybourne, and is now seen wearing a London & North Eastern Railway black livery, so can truly be referred to as a 'J15' engine, the class designation given to the locomotives following the grouping of 1923 when they were absorbed into the LNER fleet.

Above left and right: **SHERINGHAM TO WEYBOURNE** The North Norfolk line runs along a lengthy straight section between the road crossing and a cutting that marks the imminent arrival at Weybourne. Resident English Electric Type 3 No D6732 is seen shortly after passing over the bridge that crosses the road from Sheringham, then, captured from a higher vantage point, the North Sea provides a vivid backdrop as No 8572 approaches Weybourne.

Right: **SHERINGHAM TO WEYBOURNE** During its visit to the railway, Great Western 'Hall' Class 4-6-0 No 4936 *Kinlet Hall* is seen on the straight as it approaches Weybourne, with the windmill just in view in the background.

Opposite page: **SHERINGHAM TO WEYBOURNE** The Weybourne distant signal is just visible in the distance in this dramatic low-angle image of No 4936 *Kinlet Hall.*

Left: **SHERINGHAM TO WEYBOURNE** It's another blustery day with a wind off the sea strongly influencing the movement of the exhaust as visiting 9F 2-10-0 No 92214 approaches Weybourne shortly before entering the cutting.

Below left and right: **SHERINGHAM TO WEYBOURNE** Two shots of resident 9F No 92203 on mixed-goods train duties as it approaches Weybourne.

Right: **SHERINGHAM TO WEYBOURNE** 'B1' 4-6-0 No 61306 approaches Weybourne on the straight section of track, with the distant signal just visible in the background. The lineside hut adds to the overall image of steam days on the railways of Britain.

Right: **SHERINGHAM TO WEYBOURNE** Former Great Western 0-6-2T No 5619 is brought to a halt by the Weybourne outer home signal, which is set in the stop position. It is a traditional 'somersault' signal of a type that was once seen around the M&GN network. The box mounted immediately below the signal indicates the platform number to which the train is to be routed on entering Weybourne station.

Above: **SHERINGHAM TO WEYBOURNE** When the signal changes to the 'off' position, No 5619 restarts its train.

Right: **SHERINGHAM TO WEYBOURNE** The signal has also been cleared for 'Black Five' 4-6-0 No 45337, which restarts its train in order to make a Weybourne arrival.

In 2012 the 'somersault' signal was replaced by an LNER upper-quadrant example with a backing board *(inset)*. White-coloured backing boards like this were used to give the crews of approaching trains improved visibility of the signal. The platform indicator is mounted on the post below the signal arm.

Above left: **SHERINGHAM TO WEYBOURNE** The 'J15' (GER 'Y14') 0-6-0 is seen here in its British Railways guise, sporting the running number 65462 and a BR black livery, as it passes the 'somersault' signal on the approach to Weybourne.

Left: **APPROACHING WEYBOURNE** The 'Quad-Art' coaching set forms the train behind 'N2' Class 0-6-2T No 1744 as it works steadily through the cutting with Weybourne station now in sight of the footplate crew.

Above: **LEAVING WEYBOURNE** For several years 1924-built Great Eastern Railway 'N7' Class 0-6-2T No 69621 formed part of the North Norfolk Railway's fleet of working steam locomotives. No longer based at the railway, it is seen leaving Weybourne bound for Sheringham with a mixed goods train.

Weybourne

Above: **WEYBOURNE** No 1744 stands ready to depart for Holt, the climb away from Weybourne being almost immediately ahead of the 'N2'.

Above right: **WEYBOURNE** Resident 9F 2-10-0 No 92203, without its nameplates, arrives at Platform 2 with a train from Sheringham. The main station buildings are located on the facing Platform 1.

Right **WEYBOURNE** On this occasion No 92203, again nameless, stands ready to depart from Platform 1.

WEYBOURNE The Station Master looks on as No 69621 arrives at Platform 2 with its train. The signal box on the platform was once located at Holt. Just visible in this shot, the footbridge gives passenger access between the platforms and formerly stood at Stowmarket station, there never having been a footbridge here previously. Weybourne station opened in 1901 and in the past served a nearby Army camp.

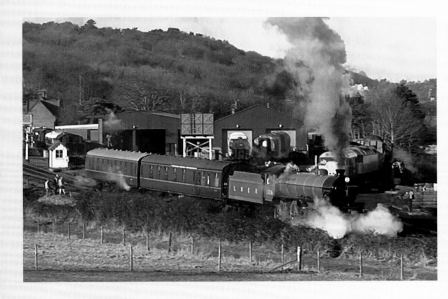

Above left: **WEYBOURNE** The former resident 'B1' 4-6-0 appears here in an LNER livery and carrying the running number 1306. It is heading for Sheringham with a short two-coach train, not very taxing for a locomotive capable of hauling much heavier trains. The buildings that form the North Norfolk Railway's Locomotive Department provide a backdrop, with a running shed and servicing and overhauling facilities.

Above right: **WEYBOURNE** During a visit to the railway, British Railways Standard Class 4 2-6-0 No 76079 prepares to depart for Holt from Platform 2. Built at Horwich in 1957, this locomotive is of the same class as the North Norfolk Railway-based 'Mogul' No 76084.

Right: **WEYBOURNE** 'N7' Class 0-6-2T No 69621 reverses off shed to take up the day's rostered operational duties hauling service trains along the 5¼-mile heritage line.

WEYBOURNE Prior to a busy day of activity on the railway, preparation is well under way outside the running shed, with no fewer than three steam locomotives seen in various stages of readiness.

Weybourne to Holt

Below: **KELLING HEATH HALT** The steepest section on the whole of the North Norfolk Railway commences just beyond Weybourne facing trains heading for Holt. A single-platform halt has been constructed here by the North Norfolk Railway in order to serve Kelling Heath Holiday Park.

Right: **KELLING HEATH HALT** Trains only stop here as they head downgrade towards Weybourne to avoid having to restart trains on the harsh 1 in 80 climb. The Great Western '5600' Class 0-6-2 tank locomotive is seen with the 'Quad-Art' coaching stock as it is about to pass the platform.

Below right: **KELLING HEATH HALT** Carrying 'The Broadsman' headboard, the resident British Railways 'Standard 4' 'Mogul' passes the halt.

WEYBOURNE TO HOLT Sporting LNER black livery, the 'J15' 0-6-0 passes the Weybourne distant signal as it makes the climb away from the station.

Right: **WEYBOURNE TO HOLT**
The North Sea is just visible in the distance as the 'N2' 0-6-2 tank locomotive draws the articulated coaching stock past the Weybourne distant signal, which is hidden by the trees and the exhaust.

Right: **WEYBOURNE TO HOLT**
The LNER-liveried 'J15' is seen here with the same train as featured on the previous page. Rounding the curve after passing the signal, the 0-6-0 starts to enter the cutting that is a feature of this location.

WEYBOURNE TO HOLT Here the 'J15' wears the British Railways black livery together with the running number 65462 that it carried following nationalisation. It is working a train through Kelling Heath cutting.

WEYBOURNE TO HOLT As trains emerge from the cutting they negotiate a level crossing that, although allowing vehicles to cross the line, is more regularly used as a pedestrian foot crossing. Resident British Railways 'Standard 4' 2-6-0 No 76084 is watched by a group of holidaymakers from the nearby Kelling Heath Holiday Park as it passes. Although not in view here, a crossing-keeper's cottage stands on the opposite side of the line.

WEYBOURNE TO HOLT Stanier 'Black Five' 4-6-0 No 45337 approaches the end of its journey, having passed the Holt distant signal, which is just in sight behind the train. The North Norfolk Railway completed the extension of its running line to its newly built Holt platform, located at High Kelling just short of the town, in 1989.

Holt

HOLT The Midland & Great Northern Joint Railway station building found on Platform 1 today once stood at Stalham on the line to Great Yarmouth. Having been dismantled brick by brick and transported to the railway and re-erected it was opened in 2004.

Left and above: **HOLT** When the railway initially began services to its new terminus, today's Platform 2, which is offset from the main platform, was the only one able to be used by passengers. The sole shelter from the elements on the platform is a 'bus shelter'-type structure typical of those once found at lineside halts around the national network.

HOLT No 76084 arrives at Holt with mixed goods train. Watering facilities are located here at the end of Platform 1. The signal box consists of the upper section of the former Midland Railway box that once stood at Upper Portland Sidings in Nottinghamshire; the lower section is constructed of concrete blocks, resembling a style once used by the M&GN.

HOLT British Railways Standard 9F 2-10-0 No 92203 arrives at Holt with a passenger train; the *Black Prince* nameplate can just be seen on the smoke deflector as the locomotive arrives at Platform 1.

HOLT The 'J15' ('Y14') 0-6-0, in Great Eastern Railway livery with the 'Quad-Art' coaches behind the tender, is about to arrive at Platform 2 with its train. The pointwork allowing trains to access Platform 1 is evident, with a siding beyond, parallel to the main running line. This siding is often used to stable goods trains that, having arrived at Platform 1, are reversed straight back into it.

HOLT The railway's 'flagship' locomotive, 1928-built Beyer Peacock 'B12' 4-6-0 No 8572, rolls into the main Platform 1 road at the end of its journey along the atmospheric North Norfolk Railway, a credit to all those who have laboured over the years to create this present-day tribute to the Midland & Great Northern Joint Railway.

Index of locomotives

Above: **SHERINGHAM** Many visitors to the North Norfolk Railway arrive and depart by the national network services from Norwich which arrive at the 'other station in town'. As can be seen from this view, showing the level crossing and the rail link to the North Norfolk Railway, the two stations are within easy walking distance of each other, The level crossing is used for occasional special trains and the transfer of rolling stock to and from the national network. *Peter Townsend*